the ULTIMATE series

PIANO • VOCAL

W9-AGU-213

TREASURY of STANDARDS
VOLUME 3 P to Z

WITHDRAWN

HAL LEONARD PUBLISHING CORPORATION

Home Office:
960 East Mark Street
Winona MN 55987

National Sales Office:
8112 West Bluemound Road
Milwaukee WI 53213

For all works contained herein:
Unauthorized copying, arranging, adapting, recording or public performance is an infringement of copyright.
Infringers are liable under the law.

TREASURY of STANDARDS
VOLUME 3 P to Z

Contents

P.S. I LOVE YOU

Words by JOHNNY MERCER
Music by GORDON JENKINS

© Copyright 1934 by La Salle Music Publishers, Inc., New York, N.Y.
© Copyright renewed 1961 and assigned to MCA Music, a division of MCA, Inc.
© Copyright renewed 1962 by Johnny Mercer d/b/a Commander Publications
International Copyright Secured   Made in U.S.A.   All Rights Reserved

MCA MUSIC

PICK YOURSELF UP

Words by DOROTHY FIELDS
Music by JEROME KERN

Copyright © 1936 T.B. Harms Company (c/o The Welk Music Group)
Copyright renewed.
International Copyright Secured   Made in U.S.A.   All Rights Reserved

PEOPLE

(From "FUNNY GIRL")

Words by BOB MERRILL
Music by JULE STYNE

Copyright © 1963 & 1964 by Bob Merrill and Jule Styne
Chappell-Styne, Inc. and Wonderful Music Corp., owners of publication and allied rights throughout the World. Chappell & Co., Inc., sole selling agent.
International Copyright Secured   ALL RIGHTS RESERVED   Printed in the U.S.A.
Unauthorized copying, arranging, adapting, recording or public performance is an infringement of copyright.
Infringers are liable under the law.

12

PEOPLE WILL SAY WE'RE IN LOVE

(From "OKLAHOMA!")

Words by OSCAR HAMMERSTEIN II
Music by RICHARD RODGERS

Copyright © 1943 by Williamson Music Co. Copyright Renewed.
Chappell & Co., Inc., sole selling agent.
International Copyright Secured   ALL RIGHTS RESERVED   Printed in the U.S.A.
Unauthorized copying, arranging, adapting, recording or public performance is an infringement of copyright.
Infringers are liable under the law.

THE PETITE WALTZ

English Lyric by E.A. ELLINGTON
and PHILLIS CLAIRE
Music by JOE HEYNE

© Copyright 1950, 1956 by World Music Company and Editions Pletnick, Brussels, Belgium
Copyright assigned to DUCHESS MUSIC CORPORATION (MCA) for all English speaking countries of the World
Copyright Renewed
International Copyright Secured   Made in U.S.A.   All Rights Reserved

MCA MUSIC

18

PICCOLO PETE

Words and Music by
PHIL BAXTER

© Copyright 1929 by MCA MUSIC, A Division of MCA Inc., New York, NY
Copyright Renewed
International Copyright Secured   Made in U.S.A.   All Rights Reserved

MCA MUSIC

22

PIGALLE

English Words by CHARLES NEWMAN
French Words by GEORGES ULMER and GEO KOGER
Music by GEORGE ULMER

© Copyright 1946, 1948 by Editions Robert Salvet, Paris, France
Sole Selling Agent MCA MUSIC, A Division of MCA Inc., New York, NY for the U.S.A. and Canada
International Copyright Secured   Made in U.S.A.   All Rights Reserved

MCA MUSIC

Theme From The Universal Picture
THE PROMISE
(I'll Never Say "Goodbye")

Words by ALAN and MARILYN BERGMAN
Music by DAVID SHIRE

Moderately, with much feeling

With pedal

Say "good-

bye?"   Why, I can bare-ly say "good-night."   If   I can hard-ly take my
bye."   We're danc-ers on a crowd-ed floor.   While oth-er danc-ers live from

eyes   from yours,   how far can I go?____   Walk a-
song   to song,   our mu-sic goes on.____   On and

© Copyright 1978 by LEEDS MUSIC CORPORATION and DUCHESS MUSIC CORPORATION, New York, NY 10022
International Copyright Secured   Made in U.S.A.   All Rights Reserved

MCA MUSIC

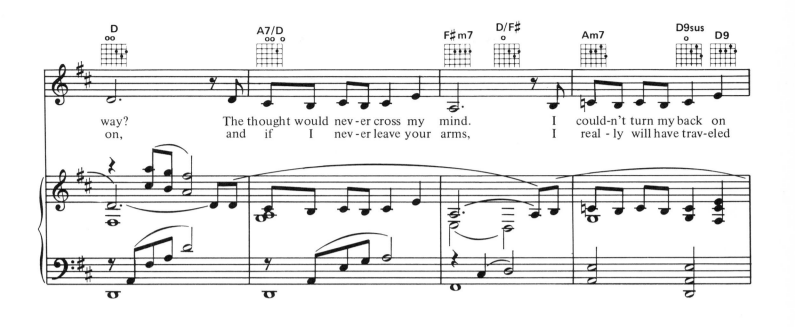

way? The thought would nev-er cross my mind. I could-n't turn my back on
on, and if I nev-er leave your arms, I real-ly will have trav-eled

spring or fall, your smile least of all. When
ev - 'ry where, for my least world is there. When

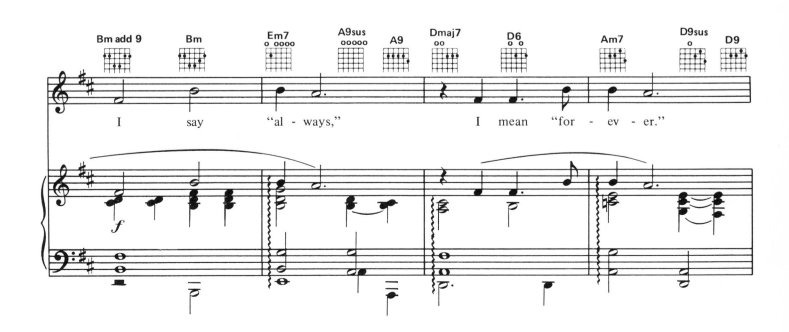

I say "al - ways," I mean "for - ev - er."

30

*Cue notes optional 2nd time.

PUPPY LOVE

Moderately slow

Words and Music by PAUL ANKA

And they called it pup-py love, _____ Oh, I guess they'll nev-er know, how a young heart real-ly feels, _____ and __ why I love her so. _____ And they called it pup-py

© Copyright 1959, 1972 by MANAGEMENT AGENCY AND MUSIC PUBLISHING INC. c/o MCA MUSIC, A Division of MCA Inc., New York, N.Y.
International Copyright Secured   Made in U.S.A.   All Rights Reserved
MCA MUSIC

QUE SERA, SERA
(WHATEVER WILL BE, WILL BE)

Words and Music by JAY LIVINGSTON
and RAY EVANS

Copyright renewed 1983 by Jay Livingston and Ray Evans
Publication rights worldwide assigned to Jay Livingston Music and St. Angelo Music
International Copyright Secured   All Rights Reserved

QUIET NIGHTS OF QUIET STARS
(Corcovado)

English Words by GENE LEES
Original Words & Music by ANTONIO CARLOS JOBIM

Moderately slow

Qui - et nights of qui - et stars, qui - et chords from my___

___ gui - tar float - ing on the si - lence that___ sur - rounds

© Copyright 1962, 1964 by Antonio Carlos Jobim, Brazil
Sole Selling Agent DUCHESS MUSIC CORPORATION (MCA), New York, NY for all English Speaking Countries
International Copyright Secured   Made in U.S.A.   All Rights Reserved

MCA MUSIC

THE RAIN IN SPAIN
(From "MY FAIR LADY")

Words by ALAN JAY LERNER
Music by FREDERICK LOEWE

Copyright © 1956 by Alan Jay Lerner & Frederick Loewe
Chappell & Co., Inc. owner of publication and allied rights throughout the World.
International Copyright Secured   ALL RIGHTS RESERVED   Printed in the U.S.A.
Unauthorized copying, arranging, adapting, recording or public performance is an infringement of copyright.
Infringers are liable under the law.

40

THE RAINBOW CONNECTION

Words and Music by
PAUL WILLIAMS and KENNY ASCHER

Copyright © 1979 WELBECK MUSIC CORP. c/o ATV MUSIC GROUP, 6255 Sunset Blvd., Los Angeles, CA 90028
All Rights Reserved

SATIN DOLL

By DUKE ELLINGTON,
JOHNNY MERCER and BILLY STRAYHORN

Copyright © 1958 by Tempo Music, Inc.
International Copyright Secured   All Rights Reserved

REMINISCING

Words and Music by GRAHAM GOBLE

With movement

Fri- day night,__ it was late.__ I was walk- in' you home. We got__ down to-
That's__ the way__ it be- gan. We were hand in hand.__ Glenn Mil-
Fri- day night,__ it was late.__ I was walk- in' you home. We got__ down to-

© 1978 American Tumbleweed Music
All rights for the U.S.A. and Canada except print controlled by Screen Gems - EMI Music, Inc., 6255 Sunset Blvd., Hollywood, CA 90028
All Rights Reserved

SAN FRANCISCO
(BE SURE TO WEAR SOME FLOWERS IN YOUR HAIR)

Words and Music by JOHN PHILLIPS

© Copyright 1967, 1970 by MCA MUSIC, A Division of MCA Inc., New York, NY
International Copyright Secured   Made in U.S.A.   All Rights Reserved
MCA MUSIC

SEA OF LOVE

Copyright © 1957, 1959 by Fort Knox Music Inc. and Trio Music Company, Inc.
All rights administered by Hudson Bay Music, Inc.
International Copyright Secured   Made in U.S.A.   All Rights Reserved
Used by Permission

SEASONS IN THE SUN
(Le Moribond)

English Lyric by ROD McKUEN
Music by JACQUES BREL

Copyright © 1961, 1964 by Societe Nouvelle des Editions Musicales TUTTI
Edward B. Marks Music Company: Sole Licensing & Selling Agent for the United States, Canada, British Commonwealth & Republic of Ireland
International Copyright Secured   Made in U.S.A.   All Rights Reserved
Used by Permission

SEEMS LIKE OLD TIMES

Words and Music by JOHN JACOB LOEB
and CARMEN LOMBARDO

Copyright © renewed 1973 Flojan Music Publishing Company
Exclusive Licensee Ahlert-Burke Corporation
International Copyright Secured   All Rights Reserved   Used by Permission

SEPTEMBER MORN

Words and Music by NEIL DIAMOND
and GILBERT BECAUD

Moderately slow

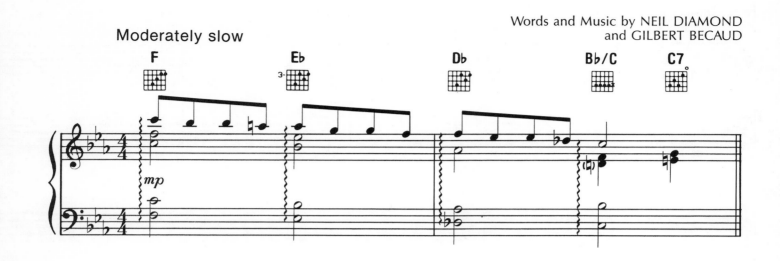

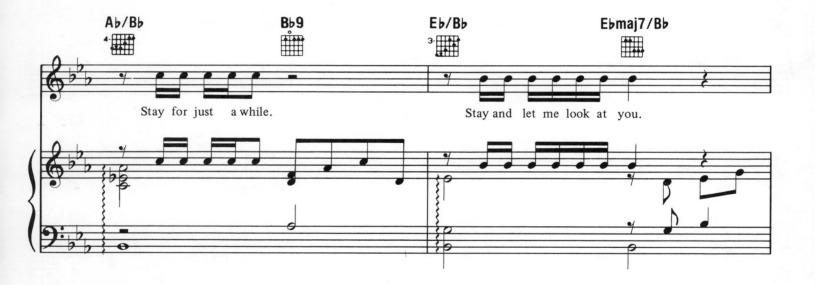

Stay for just a while. Stay and let me look at you.

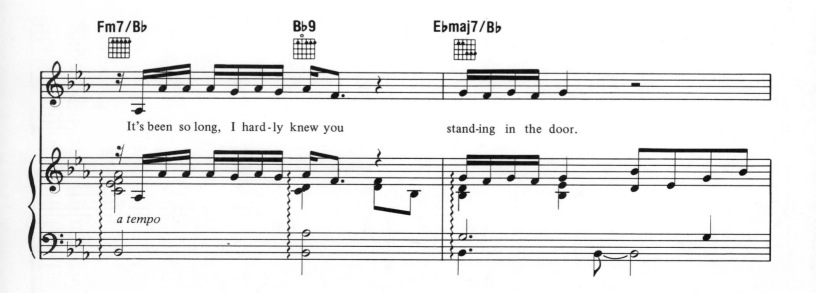

It's been so long, I hard-ly knew you standing in the door.

© 1978 STONEBRIDGE MUSIC and EMA-SUISSE
All Rights Reserved

74

SHARE YOUR LOVE WITH ME

Words and Music by DEADRIC MALONE
and AL BRAGGS

© Copyright 1963, 1981 by Music Corporation of America, Inc. New York, NY
International Copyright Secured   Made in U.S.A.   All Rights Reserved

MCA MUSIC

share _____ your love with me. _____ It's a heart - ache

when love is gone _____ and it's bad _____ and you know it's e - ven

sad _____ in thee la - ter on _____ there's no _____ one blind - er

than he who just won't see. _____ and it's a shame _____ if you don't

share _____ your love with me _____ I can't help it

SHALL WE DANCE?
(From "THE KING AND I")

Words by OSCAR HAMMERSTEIN II
Music by RICHARD RODGERS

Copyright © 1951 by Richard Rodgers and Oscar Hammerstein II. Copyright renewed.
Williamson Music Co., owner of publication and allied rights for all countries of the Western Hemisphere and Japan.
Chappell & Co., Inc., sole selling agent.
International Copyright Secured   ALL RIGHTS RESERVED   Printed in the U.S.A.
Unauthorized copying, arranging, adapting, recording or public performance is an infringement of copyright.
Infringers are liable under the law.

SHE BELIEVES IN ME

Slowly with movement

Words & Music by STEVE GIBB

Copyright © 1977 Jack and Bill Music Company
(c/o The Welk Music Group, Santa Monica, CA 90401)
International Copyright Secured   Made in U.S.A.   All Rights Reserved

THE SHEIK OF ARABY

Words by HARRY B. SMITH
and FRANCIS WHEELER
Music by TED SNYDER

O - ver the des - ert wild and free _____
While stars are fad - ing in the dawn _____

Rides the bold Shiek of Ar - a - by. _____
O - ver the des - ert they'll be gone; _____

Copyright © 1921 TED SNYDER MUSIC PUBLISHING CO.
Pursuant to Sections 304(c) and 401(b) of the U.S. Copyright Law.
International Copyright Secured   All Rights Reserved

SHRIMP BOATS

Words and Music by PAUL MASON HOWARD
and PAUL WESTON

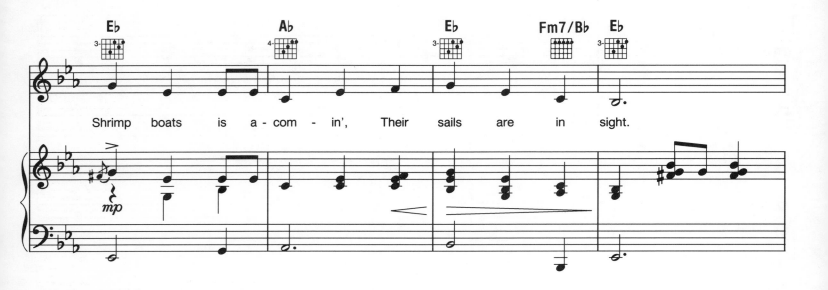

Shrimp boats is a-com - in', Their sails are in sight.

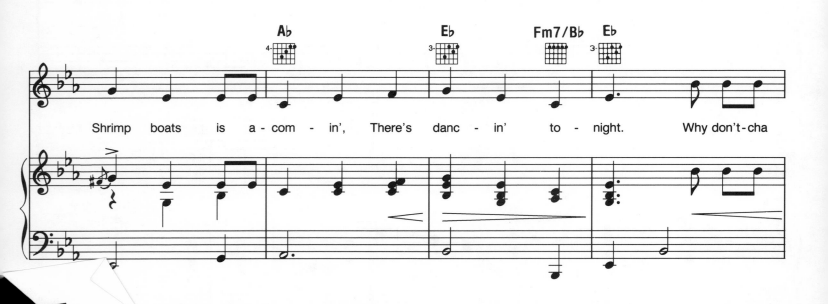

Shrimp boats is a-com - in', There's danc - in' to - night. Why don't-cha

© 1951 WALT DISNEY MUSIC COMPANY Copyright Renewed
International Copyright Secured   Made in U.S.A.   All Rights Reserved

SINCERELY

Words and Music by HARVEY FUQUA
and ALAN FREED

Copyright © 1954 (Renewed) Arc Music Corporation, 110 East 59th Street, New York, N.Y. 10022
International Copyright Secured   Made in U.S.A.   All Rights Reserved

SO NICE
(SUMMER SAMBA)

Original Words and Music by MARCOS VALLE
and PAULO SERGIO VALLE
English Words by NORMAN GIMBEL

Relaxed Bossa Nova

Some-one to hold me tight, that would be ver-y nice Some-one to love me right, that would be ver-y nice. Some-one to un-der-stand each lit-tle dream __ in me, some-one to take my hand, to be a team __ with me. So nice, _____

© Copyright 1965, 1966 by Marcos Valle and Paulo Sergio Valle
Sole Selling Agent MCA MUSIC, A Division of MCA Inc., New York, NY
International Copyright Secured   Made in U.S.A.   All Rights Reserved

MCA MUSIC

SMALL WORLD
(From "GYPSY")

Words by STEPHEN SONDHEIM
Music by JULE STYNE

Copyright © 1959 by Norbeth Productions, Inc., and Stephen Sondheim
Williamson Music Co. and Stratford Music Corp., owners of publication and allied rights throughout the World
(Chappell & Co., Inc., Administrator)
International Copyright Secured   ALL RIGHTS RESERVED   Printed in the U.S.A.
Unauthorized copying, arranging, adapting, recording or public performance is an infringement of copyright.
Infringers are liable under the law.

SMOKE GETS IN YOUR EYES

(From "ROBERTA")

Words by OTTO HARBACH
Music by JEROME KERN

Copyright © 1933 T.B. Harms Company (c/o The Welk Music Group, Santa Monica, CA 90401)
Copyright renewed.
International Copyright Secured   Made in U.S.A.   All Rights Reserved

103

SOME ENCHANTED EVENING

(From "SOUTH PACIFIC")

Words by OSCAR HAMMERSTEIN II
Music by RICHARD RODGERS

Copyright © 1949 by Richard Rodgers and Oscar Hammerstein II. Copyright renewed.
Williamson Music Co., owner of publication and allied rights for all countries of the Western Hemisphere and Japan.
Chappell & Co., Inc., sole selling agent.
International Copyright Secured   ALL RIGHTS RESERVED   Printed in the U.S.A.
Unauthorized copying, arranging, adapting, recording or public performance is an infringement of copyright.
Infringers are liable under the law.

105

SOMEDAY
(You'll Want Me To Want You)

Words and Music by JIMMIE HODGES

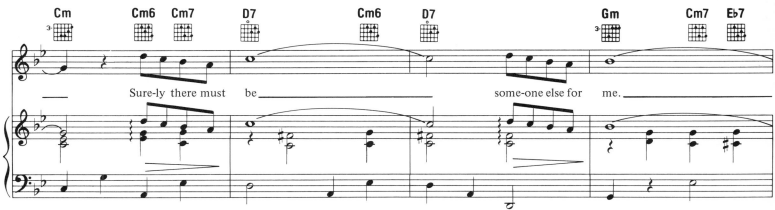

© Copyright 1940, 1944 by DUCHESS MUSIC CORPORATION, New York, NY
Copyright Renewed
Rights Administered by MCA MUSIC, A Division of MCA Inc., New York, NY
International Copyright Secured   Made in U.S.A.   All Rights Reserved

MCA MUSIC

SOMEWHERE IN TIME

By JOHN BARRY

© Copyright 1980 by DUCHESS MUSIC CORPORATION
Rights Administered by MCA MUSIC, A Division of MCA INC., New York, NY 10022
International Copyright Secured   Made in U.S.A.   All Rights Reserved

MCA MUSIC

SONG SUNG BLUE

Words and Music by NEIL DIAMOND

© 1972 PROPHET MUSIC, INC.
All Rights Reserved

SOON IT'S GONNA RAIN

(From "THE FANTASTICKS")

Words by TOM JONES
Music by HARVEY SCHMIDT

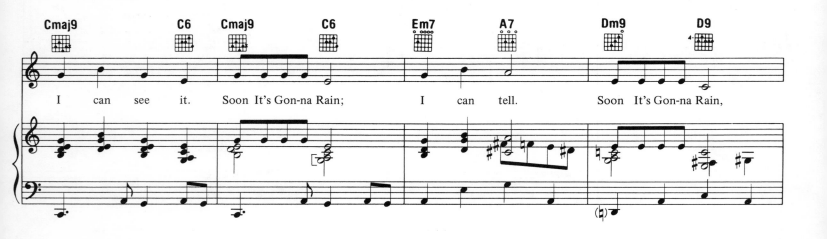

Copyright © 1960 by Tom Jones and Harvey Schmidt
Chappell & Co., Inc., Owner of publication and allied rights
International Copyright Secured   ALL RIGHTS RESERVED   Printed in the U.S.A.
Unauthorized copying, arranging, adapting, recording or public performance is an infringement of copyright.
Infringers are liable under the law.

STRANGERS IN THE NIGHT

Words by CHARLES SINGLETON
and EDDIE SNYDER
Music by BERT KAEMPFERT

© Copyright 1966 by Champion Music Corporation and Screen Gems-EMI
Sole Selling Agent MCA MUSIC, A Division of MCA Inc., New York, NY
International Copyright Secured   Made in U.S.A.   All Rights Reserved

MCA MUSIC

THE SOUND OF MUSIC
(From "THE SOUND OF MUSIC")

Words by OSCAR HAMMERSTEIN II
Music by RICHARD RODGERS

The hills are a-live with the sound of mu - sic, ____

With songs they have sung for a thou - sand

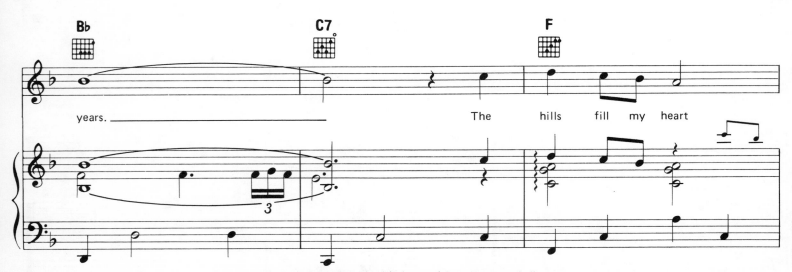

years. ____ The hills fill my heart

Copyright © 1959 by Richard Rodgers and Oscar Hammerstein II
Williamson Music Co., owner of publication and allied rights throughout the Western Hemisphere and Japan. Chappell & Co., Inc., sole selling agent.
International Copyright Secured   ALL RIGHTS RESERVED   Printed in the U.S.A.
Unauthorized copying, arranging, adapting, recording or public performance is an infringement of copyright.
Infringers are liable under the law.

STRANGE MUSIC

Based on "Nocturne" & "Wedding Day In Troldhaugen" by EDVARD GRIEG
Musical Adaption by ROBERT WRIGHT & GEORGE FORREST

Copyright © 1944 by Chappell & Co., Inc. Copyright Renewed.
International Copyright Secured   ALL RIGHTS RESERVED   Printed in the U.S.A.
Unauthorized copying, arranging, adapting, recording or public performance is an infringement of copyright.
Infringers are liable under the law.

SUGAR BLUES

Words by LUCY FLETCHER
Music by CLARENCE WILLIAMS

© Copyright 1919 by MCA MUSIC, A Division of MCA Inc., New York, NY
Copyright Renewed
International Copyright Secured   Made in U.S.A.   All Rights Reserved
MCA MUSIC

132

SUMMERTIME IN VENICE

English Words by
CARL SIGMAN
Music by ICINI

© Copyright 1955, 1959 by MCA MUSIC, A Division of MCA Inc., New York, NY
International Copyright Secured   Made in U.S.A.   All Rights Reserved
MCA MUSIC

134

A SUNDAY KIND OF LOVE

Words and Music by BARBARA BELLE,
LOUIS PRIMA, ANITA LEONARD and STAN RHODES

© Copyright 1946, 1972 by MCA MUSIC, A Division of MCA Inc., New York, NY
Copyright Renewed
International Copyright Secured   Made in U.S.A.   All Rights Reserved
MCA MUSIC

137

SUNRISE, SUNSET
(From the Musical "FIDDLER ON THE ROOF")

Words by SHELDON HARNICK
Music by JERRY BOCK

Copyright © 1964 by Alley Music Corporation and Trio Music Company, Inc.
All rights administered by Hudson Bay Music, Inc.
International Copyright Secured   Made in U.S.A.   All Rights Reserved
Used by Permission

141

SUNRISE SERENADE

Lyric by JACK LAWRENCE
Music by FRANKIE CARLE

Copyright © 1938 (renewed) Dorsey Bros. Music, Inc., a division of Music Sales Corp., 24, E. 22nd Street, New York, NY 10010
International Copyright Secured   Made in U.S.A.   All Rights Reserved

THE SURREY WITH THE FRINGE ON TOP

(From "OKLAHOMA!")

Words by OSCAR HAMMERSTEIN II
Music by RICHARD RODGERS

Copyright © 1943 by Williamson Music Co.   Copyright Renewed.
Chappell & Co., Inc., sole selling agent.
International Copyright Secured   ALL RIGHTS RESERVED   Printed in the U.S.A.
Unauthorized copying, arranging, adapting, recording or public performance is an infringement of copyright.
Infringers are liable under the law.

SWEET CAROLINE

Words and Music by NEIL DIAMOND

Moderately, very steady

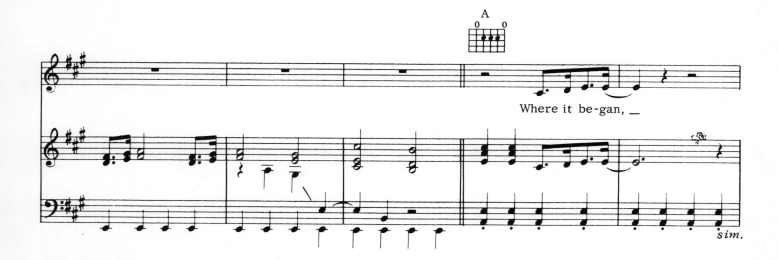

Where it be-gan, __

I can't be-gin to know-in,' but then I know it's grow-in'

© 1969 STONEBRIDGE MUSIC
All Rights Reserved

151

SWEET SURRENDER

Words and Music by
JOHN DENVER

© 1974 WALT DISNEY MUSIC COMPANY
International Copyright Secured   Made in U.S.A.   All Rights Reserved

154

THE SWEETEST SOUNDS

(From "NO STRINGS")

Words and Music by
RICHARD RODGERS

Copyright © 1962 by Richard Rodgers
Williamson Music Co., owner of publication and allied rights for all countries of the Western Hemisphere and Japan.
Chappell & Co., Inc., sole selling agent.
International Copyright Secured   ALL RIGHTS RESERVED   Printed in the U.S.A.
Unauthorized copying, arranging, adapting, recording or public performance is an infringement of copyright.
Infringers are liable under the law.

THAT'S ALL

Words and Music by ALAN BRANDT
and BOB HAYMES

© 1952 Renewed 1982 Mixed Bag Music, Inc.
All Rights Reserved.   Used By Permission.

TAKES TWO TO TANGO

Words and Music by AL HOFFMAN
and DICK MANNING

Copyright © 1952, renewed, Jewel Music Publishing Co., Inc., New York, NY 10022
International Copyright Secured   Made in U.S.A.   All Rights Reserved

165

Additional Verses

3. You can haunt any house by yourself,
   Be a man, or a mouse by yourself;
   You can act like a King on a throne,
   There are lots of things that you can do alone! But!!! "TAKES TWO TO TANGO" etc.

4. You can fight like a champ by yourself,
   You can lick any stamp by yourself;
   You can be very brave on the 'phone,
   There are lots of things that you can do alone! But!!! "TAKES TWO TO TANGO" etc.

5. You can bark like a dog by yourself,
   Or get lost in a fog by yourself;
   You can hoot like an owl on your own,
   There are lots of things that you can do alone! But!!! "TAKES TWO TO TANGO" etc.

6. You can get very old by yourself,
   Catch a fish, or a cold by yourself;
   Dig a ditch, strike it rich on your own,
   There are lots of things that you can do alone! But!!! "TAKES TWO TO TANGO" etc.

THANK HEAVEN FOR LITTLE GIRLS

(From "GIGI")

Words by ALAN JAY LERNER
Music by FREDERICK LOEWE

Copyright © 1957 & 1958 by Chappell & Co., Inc.
International Copyright Secured   ALL RIGHTS RESERVED   Printed in the U.S.A.
Unauthorized copying, arranging, adapting, recording or public performance is an infringement of copyright.
Infringers are liable under the law.

THAT'S ENTERTAINMENT
(From "THE BAND WAGON")

Words by HOWARD DIETZ
Music by ARTHUR SCHWARTZ

1. The clown with his pants fall-ing down,
2. The doubt while the ju-ry is out,

Or the dance that's a dream of ro-mance,
Or the thrill when a they're read-ing ro-the mance, will,

Or the scene where the vil-lain is mean;
Or the chase for the man with the face;

That's en-en-ter-tain-ment!
That's en-en-ter-tain-ment!

Copyright © 1953 by Chappell & Co., Inc. Copyright renewed.
International Copyright Secured   ALL RIGHTS RESERVED   Printed in the U.S.A.
Unauthorized copying, arranging, adapting, recording or public performance is an infringement of copyright.
Infringers are liable under the law.

173

THAT'S LIFE

Words and Music by DEAN KAY
and KELLY GORDON

Copyright © 1964, 1966 Bibo Music Publishers (c/o The Welk Music Group, Santa Monica, CA 90401)
International Copyright Secured   Made in U.S.A.   All Rights Reserved

175

THERE MUST BE A WAY

Words and Music by SAMMY GALLOP
and DAVID SAXON

Copyright © 1945 by Laurel Music Corporation.   Copyright Renewed.
Copyright assigned in the U.S. to Range Road Music Inc., Quartet Music Inc., and Sammy Gallop Music Co.
Copyright assigned outside the U.S. to Range Road Music Inc. and Quartet Music Inc.
All rights for Range Road Music Inc. and Quartet Music Inc. administered by Herald Square Music Inc.
International Copyright Secured   Made in U.S.A.   All Rights Reserved
Used by Permission

THEY CALL THE WIND MARIA

(From "PAINT YOUR WAGON")

Words by ALAN JAY LERNER
Music by FREDERICK LOEWE

Lively

Copyright © 1951 by Alan Jay Lerner and Frederick Loewe
Copyright Renewed, Chappell & Co., Inc., owner of publication and allied rights throughout the World
International Copyright Secured   ALL RIGHTS RESERVED   Printed in the U.S.A.
Unauthorized copying, arranging, adapting, recording or public performance is an infringement of copyright.
Infringers are liable under the law.

THEY'RE PLAYING MY SONG
(From "THEY'RE PLAYING OUR SONG")

Words by CAROLE BAYER SAGER
Music by MARVIN HAMLISCH

Copyright © 1979, 1980 by Chappell & Co., Inc., Red Bullet Music, Unichappell Music, Inc. & Begonia Melodies, Inc.
Publication and allied rights Administered by Chappell & Co., Inc. and Unichappell Music, Inc. throughout the World.
International Copyright Secured   ALL RIGHTS RESERVED   Printed in the U.S.A.
Unauthorized copying, arranging, adapting, recording or public performance is an infringement of copyright.
Infringers are liable under the law.

own hum- ble way___ ev- 'ry per- fect note of that was writ- ten by me.

Ah, ha, they're play-ing my song,___ that ta- ble's hum-ming a- long.___ That cou- ple half out the door___

___ is com-ing back to hear more___ of my mu- sic. At first, I thought this place was a dive.___

I chose it in haste,__ but they showed they got taste,___ as long as they're play- ing my

song. Who would have known,__ nine months a- go,__ I would give birth___ at

8ba

THEY DIDN'T BELIEVE ME

Words by HERBERT REYNOLDS
Music by JEROME KERN

Copyright © 1914 T.B. Harms Company (c/o The Welk Music Group, Santa Monica, CA 90401)
Copyright renewed.
International Copyright Secured   Made in U.S.A.   All Rights Reserved

THIS CAN'T BE LOVE

(From "THE BOYS FROM SYRACUSE")

Words by LORENZ HART
Music by RICHARD RODGERS

Copyright © 1938 by Chappell & Co., Inc. Copyright Renewed.
International Copyright Secured   ALL RIGHTS RESERVED   Printed in the U.S.A.
Unauthorized copying, arranging, adapting, recording or public performance is an infringement of copyright.
Infringers are liable under the law.

THIS IS MY SONG

(From Charles Chaplin's "A COUNTESS FROM HONG KONG" a Universal Release)

By CHARLES CHAPLIN

© Copyright 1966, 1967 by MCA MUSIC, A Division of MCA Inc., New York, NY
International Copyright Secured   Made in U.S.A.   All Rights Reserved

MCA MUSIC

THOROUGHLY MODERN MILLIE

(From Ross Hunter's "THOROUGHLY MODERN MILLIE" - A Universal Picture)

Words by SAMMY CAHN
Music by JAMES VAN HEUSEN

© Coyright 1967 by Northern Music Company, New York, NY
Rights Administered by MCA Music, a division of MCA, Inc., New York, NY
International Copyright Secured   Made in U.S.A.   All Rights Reserved

MCA MUSIC

195

TOGETHER WHEREVER WE GO

(From "GYPSY")

Words by STEPHEN SONDHEIM
Music by JULE STYNE

Copyright © 1959 by Norbeth Productions, Inc. and Stephen Sondheim
Williamson Music Co. and Stratford Music Corp., Owners of publication and allied rights for the Western Hemisphere.
Chappell & Co., Inc., Administrator.
International Copyright Secured   ALL RIGHTS RESERVED   Printed in the U.S.A.
Unauthorized copying, arranging, adapting, recording or public performance is an infringement of copyright.
Infringers are liable under the law.

198

TURN AROUND

Words and Music by NEIL DIAMOND,
BURT BACHARACH and CAROLE BAYER SAGER

© 1984 STONEBRIDGE MUSIC, NEW HIDDEN VALLEY MUSIC and CAROLE BAYER SAGER MUSIC
All Rights Reserved

UNDECIDED

Words by SID ROBIN
Music by CHARLES SHAVERS

© Copyright 1939 by MCA MUSIC, A Division of MCA Inc., New York, NY
Copyright Renewed
International Copyright Secured   Made in U.S.A.   All Rights Reserved
MCA MUSIC

207

WAND'RIN' STAR
(From "PAINT YOUR WAGON")

Words by ALAN JAY LERNER
Music by FREDERICK LOEWE

Copyright © 1951 by Alan Jay Lerner & Frederick Loewe. Copyright Renewed.
Chappell & Co., Inc., owner of publication and allied rights throughout the World
International Copyright Secured   ALL RIGHTS RESERVED   Printed in the U.S.A.
Unauthorized copying, arranging, adapting, recording or public performance is an infringement of copyright.
Infringers are liable under the law.

WATCH WHAT HAPPENS

English Words by NORMAN GIMBEL
Music by MICHEL LEGRAND

Copyright © 1964 Productions Michel Legrand & Productions Francis Lemarque.
Copyright © 1965 Vogue Music & Jonware Music (c/o The Welk Music Group, Santa Monica, CA 90401)
International Copyright Secured   Made in U.S.A.   All Rights Reserved

THE WAY YOU LOOK TONIGHT

Words by DOROTHY FIELDS
Music by JEROME KERN

Copyright © 1936 T.B. Harms Company (c/o The Welk Music Group, Santa Monica, CA 90401)
Copyright renewed.
International Copyright Secured   Made in U.S.A.   All Rights Reserved

THE WAYWARD WIND

Words and Music by HERB NEWMAN
and STAN LEBOWSKY

Copyright © 1955, 1956 Bibo Music Publishers (c/o The Welk Music Group, Santa Monica, CA 90401) Copyright Renewed
International Copyright Secured   Made in U.S.A.   All Rights Reserved

WELCOME TO MY WORLD

By RAY WINKLER
and JOHN HATHCOCK

Copyright © 1961, 1964 by Tree Publishing Co., Inc. and Neilrae Music Co., 8 Music Square West, Nashville, TN 37203
This arrangement Copyright © 1984 by Tree Publishing Co., and Neilrae Music Co.
International Copyright Secured   Made in U.S.A.   All Rights Reserved

WHEN I NEED YOU

Moderately, with feeling

Words by CAROLE BAYER SAGER
Music by ALBERT HAMMOND

Copyright © 1976 & 1977 by Unichappell Music, Inc., Begonia Melodies Inc., April Music Inc., R & M Music, Inc. and Stranger Music, Inc.
Administered by Unichappell Music, Inc. and April Music, Inc. in the U.S.A. and Canada
International Copyright Secured   ALL RIGHTS RESERVED   Printed in the U.S.A.
Unauthorized copying, arranging, adapting, recording or public performance is an infringement of copyright.
Infringers are liable under the law.

WHEN I'M NOT NEAR THE GIRL I LOVE

(From "FINIAN'S RAINBOW")

Words by E.Y. Harburg
Music by Burton Lane

Copyright © 1946 by The Players Music Corp. Copyright Renewed.
Chappell & Co., Inc. sole selling agent
International Copyright Secured   ALL RIGHTS RESERVED   Printed in the U.S.A.
Unauthorized copying, arranging, adapting, recording or public performance is an infringement of copyright.
Infringers are liable under the law.

WHEN MY BABY SMILES AT ME

By HARRY VON TILZER, ANDREW B. STERLING,
BILL MUNRO and TED LEWIS

Copyright © 1920 Harry Von Tilzer Music Publishing Company (c/o The Welk Music Group, Santa Monica, CA 90401)
Copyright renewed.
International Copyright Secured   Made in U.S.A.   All Rights Reserved

WHO?

Words by OTTO HARBACH and OSCAR HAMMERSTEIN II
Music by JEROME KERN

Copyright © 1925 T.B. Harms Company (c/o The Welk Music Group, Santa Monica, CA 90401)
Copyright renewed.
International Copyright Secured   Made in U.S.A.   All Rights Reserved

WHO CAN I TURN TO
(When Nobody Needs Me)
(From the Musical Production "THE ROAR OF THE GREASEPAINT - THE SMELL OF THE CROWD")

Words and Music by LESLIE BRICUSSE
and ANTHONY NEWLEY

© Copyright 1964 Concord Music Ltd., London, England
TRO - Musical Comedy Productions, Inc., New York, controls all publication rights for the U.S.A. & Canada
International Copyright Secured   Made in U.S.A.
All Rights Reserved Including Public Performance For Profit
Used by Permission

WHO'S SORRY NOW

Words by BERT KALMER & HARRY RUBY
Music by TED SNYDER

Copyright © 1923 HARRY RUBY MUSIC & TED SNYDER MUSIC PUBLISHING CO.
Pursuant to Sections 304(c) and 401(b) of the U.S. Copyright Law.
International Copyright Secured   All Rights Reserved

240

WITH A LITTLE BIT OF LUCK
(From "MY FAIR LADY")

Words by ALAN JAY LERNER
Music by FREDERICK LOEWE

Copyright © 1956 by Alan Jay Lerner & Frederick Loewe
Chappell & Co., Inc., owner of publication and allied rights throughout the World.
International Copyright Secured   ALL RIGHTS RESERVED   Printed in the U.S.A.
Unauthorized copying, arranging, adapting, recording or public performance is an infringement of copyright.
Infringers are liable under the law.

243

WHY DO I LOVE YOU?

Words by OSCAR HAMMERSTEIN II
Music by JEROME KERN

Copyright © 1927 T.B. Harms Company (c/o The Welk Music Group, Santa Monica, CA 90401)
Copyright renewed.
International Copyright Secured   Made in U.S.A.   All Rights Reserved

WISH YOU WERE HERE
(From the musical "WISH YOU WERE HERE")

Words and Music by HAROLD ROME

Copyright © 1952 by Harold Rome
Copyright renewed, assigned to Chappell & Co., Inc.
International Copyright Secured   ALL RIGHTS RESERVED   Printed in the U.S.A.
Unauthorized copying, arranging, adapting, recording or public performance is an infringement of copyright.
Infringers are liable under the law.

A WONDERFUL GUY

(From "SOUTH PACIFIC")

Words by OSCAR HAMMERSTEIN II
Music by RICHARD RODGERS

Copyright © 1949, by Richard Rodgers and Oscar Hammerstein II, Copyright Renewed.
Williamson Music Co., owner of publication and allied rights for all countries of the Western Hemisphere and Japan.
Chappell & Co., Inc. sole selling agent.
International Copyright Secured   ALL RIGHTS RESERVED   Printed in the U.S.A.
Unauthorized copying, arranging, adapting, recording or public performance is an infringement of copyright.
Infringers are liable under the law.

YESTERDAYS

Words by OTTO HARBACH
Music by JEROME KERN

Copyright © 1933 T.B. Harms Company (c/o The Welk Music Group, Santa Monica, CA 90401)
Copyright renewed.
International Copyright Secured   Made in U.S.A.   All Rights Reserved

THE WONDERFUL WORLD OF THE YOUNG

Words and Music by SID TEPPER
and ROY C. BENNETT

*Chord names and diagrams for guitar.

© Copyright 1961 by MCA MUSIC, A Division of MCA Inc., New York, NY
International Copyright Secured   Made in U.S.A.   All Rights Reserved
MCA MUSIC

WOULDN'T IT BE LOVERLY

(From "MY FAIR LADY")

Words by ALAN JAY LERNER
Music by FREDERICK LOEWE

Copyright © 1956 by Alan Jay Lerner and Frederick Loewe.
Chappell & Co., Inc., owner of publication and allied rights throughout the world.
International Copyright Secured   ALL RIGHTS RESERVED   Printed in the U.S.A.
Unauthorized copying, arranging, adapting, recording or public performance is an infringement of copyright.
Infringers are liable under the law.

WUNDERBAR
(From "KISS ME, KATE")

Words and Music by COLE PORTER

Copyright © 1948 by Cole Porter
Copyright Renewed, Assigned to John F. Wharton, Trustee of the Cole Porter Musical & Literary Property Trusts
Chappell & Co., Inc., owner of publication and allied rights throughout the World.
International Copyright Secured   ALL RIGHTS RESERVED   Printed in the U.S.A.
Unauthorized copying, arranging, adapting, recording or public performance is an infringement of copyright.
Infringers are liable under the law.

YEARNING

Words and Music by
BENNY DAVIS and JOE BURKE

Copyright © 1925 by BOURNE CO.
Copyright Renewed 1952 Assigned to World Music Inc., P.O. Box 1319, Fair Lawn, NJ 07410
International Copyright Secured   Made in U.S.A.   All Rights Reserved

YESTERDAY'S SONGS

Words and Music by
NEIL DIAMOND

© 1981 STONEBRIDGE MUSIC
All Rights Reserved

YOU CAME A LONG WAY FROM ST. LOUIS

Words by BOB RUSSELL
Music by JOHN BENSON BROOKS

© 1948 Jewel Music Publ. Co., New York, NY
© 1976 Harrison Music Corp., Los Angeles, CA
International Copyright Secured   Made in U.S.A.   All Rights Reserved

YOU DON'T BRING ME FLOWERS

Words by NEIL DIAMOND, MARILYN BERGMAN,
and ALAN BERGMAN
Music by NEIL DIAMOND

© 1977 STONEBRIDGE MUSIC and THREESOME MUSIC
All Rights Reserved

271

274

YOU'D BE SO NICE TO COME HOME TO
(From "SOMETHING TO SHOUT ABOUT")

Words and Music by COLE PORTER

Rather Slow with Feeling

You'd be

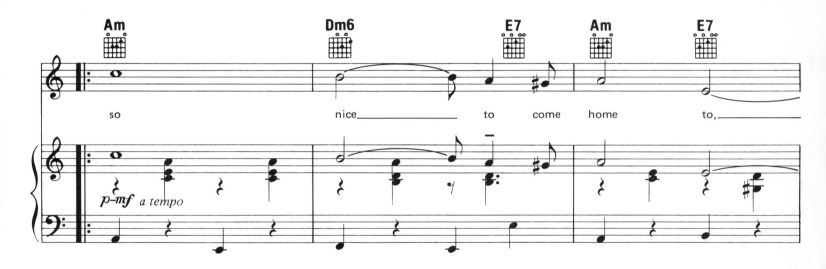

so   nice_____ to come home to,_____

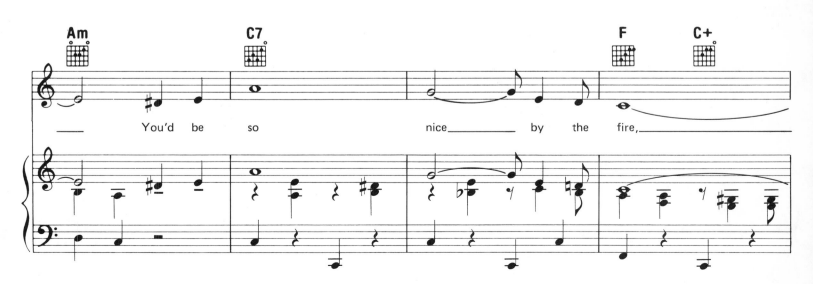

_____ You'd be so   nice_____ by the fire,_____

Copyright © 1942 by Chappell & Co., Inc. Copyright Renewed.
International Copyright Secured   ALL RIGHTS RESERVED   Printed in the U.S.A.
Unauthorized copying, arranging, adapting, recording or public performance is an infringement of copyright.
Infringers are liable under the law.

YOU PUT THE BEAT IN MY HEART

Fast Country Rock beat

Words and Music by DON PFRIMMER
and RICK GILES

thought it might be the gui-tar, I thought it might be the drums,___ or may-be some-bod-y out in the hall___ snap-pin' thumbs.___ When I

Copyright © 1983 DEJAMUS INC./MALLVEN MUSIC, INC./COTTONPATCH MUSIC, 24 Music Square East, Nashville, TN 37203
International Copyright Secured   Made in U.S.A.   All Rights Reserved

You'll Never Walk Alone
(From "CAROUSEL")

Words by OSCAR HAMMERSTEIN II
Music by RICHARD RODGERS

Copyright © 1945 Williamson Music Co.   Copyright Renewed.
Sole Selling Agent — T.B. Harms Company (c/o The Welk Music Group, Santa Monica, CA 90401)
International Copyright Secured   Made in U.S.A.   All Rights Reserved

ZIP-A-DEE-DOO-DAH

(From Walt Disney's "SONG OF THE SOUTH")

Words by RAY GILBERT
Music by ALLIE WRUBEL

© 1945 WALT DISNEY MUSIC COMPANY
Copyright Renewed
International Copyright Secured   Made in U.S.A.   All Rights Reserved

YOUNGER THAN SPRINGTIME
(From "SOUTH PACIFIC")

Words by OSCAR HAMMERSTEIN II
Music by RICHARD RODGERS

Copyright © 1949 by Richard Rodgers and Oscar Hammerstein II. Copyright Renewed.
Williamson Music Co., owner of publication and allied rights for all countries of the Western Hemisphere and Japan. Chappell & Co., Inc., sole selling agent.
International Copyright Secured   ALL RIGHTS RESERVED   Printed in the U.S.A.
Unauthorized copying, arranging, adapting, recording or public performance is an infringement of copyright.
Infringers are liable under the law.